Can

Illustrated by Dianne Stuchbury

A LITTLE LION
Oxford · Batavia · Sydney

yeasty bread

creamy butter

mellow cheese

sunwarmed tomatoes

glowing golden peaches

ripe red strawberries

tangy oranges

warm chocolate

spicy cinnamon

summer flowers?

All the different smells and tastes

help animals find their food.

Dear God
thank you for good smells
and sweet tastes
and food to eat.

Copyright © 1991 Lion Publishing
Illustrations copyright © 1991 Dianne Stuchbury

Published by
Lion Publishing plc
Sandy Lane West, Oxford, England
ISBN 0 7459 2092 6
Lion Publishing Corporation
1705 Hubbard Avenue, Batavia, Illinois 60510, USA
ISBN 0 7459 2092 6
Albatross Books Pty Ltd
PO Box 320, Sutherland, NSW 2232, Australia
ISBN 0 7324 0454 1

First published 1991
All rights reserved

Printed and bound in Yugoslavia